ODORI
Japanese Dance

Intended to provide foreigners with a brief but detailed introduction to different forms of Japanese dance, this volume illustrated with period photographs is one of a series of short works on different aspects culture prepared by the Japanese Tourist Board in the 1930's. The formal, highly stylised Noh performances and the more dramatic, quick-moving Kabuki, the Japanese dance-drama forms most familiar to westerners, are but two in a larger repertoire outlined here that include the artistic Bugaku dance performed only at the Imperial Court and at Shinto shrines during festivals, other Shinto and Buddhist dances, rural folk dances and new dance forms including western style dances. After dealing with the mythical origins and historical development of dance, the author concentrates on Kabuki, setting out the varieties of Kabuki dance, and dealing with Kabuki music and presentation. Stage and set details are also given, along with a description of the dynasties of actor-dancers who dominated Kabuki, and of the choreographers and their schools. Of particular interest to the dance historian is the section on the effect of Meiji modernisation, which led to a demand for new dance forms to represent the national life of a new age. The results were new types of Kabuki, little-known forms of Japanese modern dance, and revue shows such as the famous Takarazuka. This is a fascinating survey of an art at Japan's cultural heart.

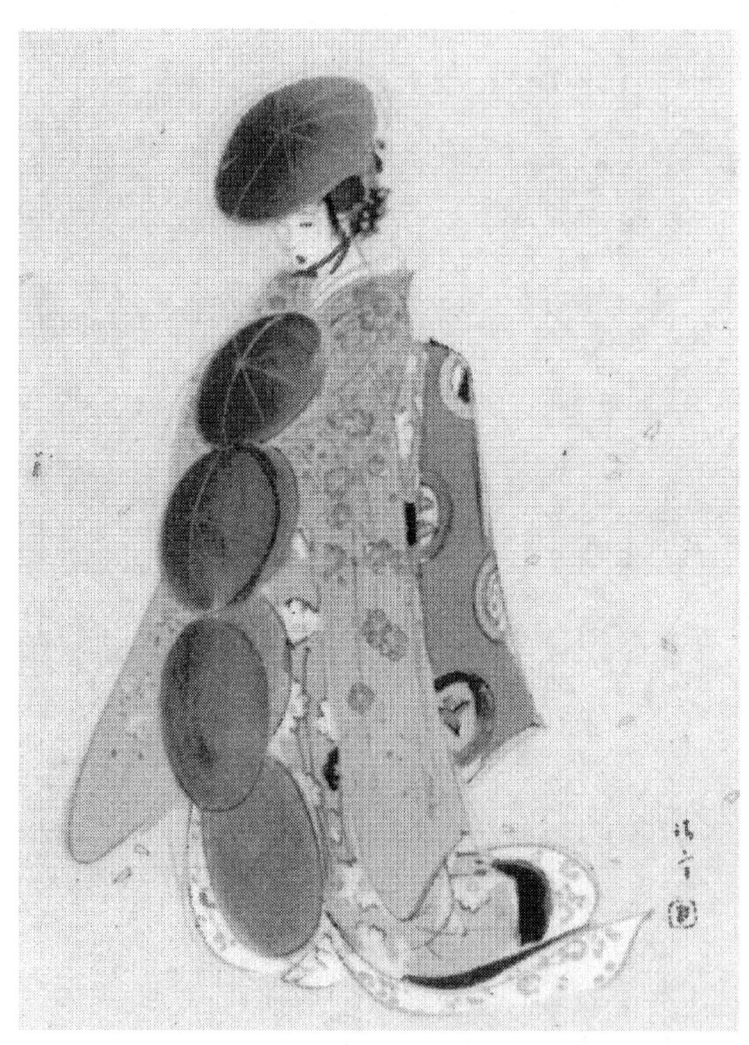

"MUSUME DOZYOZI," A POPULAR KABUKI DANCE

By Kiyokata Kaburagi

ODORI
JAPANESE DANCE

BY
KASYO MATIDA

LONDON AND NEW YORK

First published in 1938 by Board of Tourist Industry, Japanese Government Railways.

This edition first published in 2009 by
Routledge
2 Park Square, Milton Park, Abingdon, Oxfordshire OX14 4RN

Simultaneously published in the USA and Canada
by Routledge
711 Third Avenue, New York, NY 10017, USA

First issued in paperback 2016

Routledge is an imprint of the Taylor & Francis Group, an informa business

© Board of Tourist Industry, Japanese Government Railways 1938

All rights reserved. No part of this book may be reprinted or reproduced or utilised in any form or by any electronic, mechanical, or other means, now known or hereafter invented, including photocopying and recording, or in any information storage or retrieval system, without permission in writing from the publishers.

British Library Cataloguing in Publication Data
A catalogue record for this book is available from the British Library

ISBN 13: 978-1-138-97740-2 (pbk)
ISBN 13: 978-0-7103-1019-4 (hbk)

Publisher's Note
The publisher has gone to great lengths to ensure the quality of this reprint but points out that some imperfections in the original copies may be apparent. The publisher has made every effort to contact original copyright holders and would welcome correspondence from those they have been unable to trace.

EDITORIAL NOTE

It is a common desire among tourists to learn something of the culture of the countries they visit, as well as to see their beautiful scenery. To see is naturally easier than to learn, but flying visits merely for sightseeing furnish neither the time nor opportunity for more than a passing acquaintance with the culture of any foreign people. This is specially true of Japan and her people.

The Board of Tourist Industry recognizes both the obligation and the difficulty of providing foreign tourists with accurate information regarding the various phases of Japan's culture. It is, therefore, endeavouring to meet this obligation, as far as possible, by publishing this series of brochures.

The present series will, when completed, consist of more than a hundred volumes, each dealing with a different subject, but all co-ordinated. By studying the entire series, the foreign student of Japan will gain an adequate knowledge of the unique culture that has evolved in this country through the ages.

                    Board of Tourist Industry,
                    Japanese Government Railways.

NOTE

The Japanese Government has adopted a new system of spelling for certain Romanized Japanese syllable sounds. Though the spelling has been modified, the pronunciation remains the same. The modified spelling is given below with the old phonetic spelling in brackets:

    si (shi)
    ti (chi)   tu (tsu)
    hu (fu)
    zi (ji)
    sya (sha)   syu (shu)   syo (sho)
    tya (cha)   tyu (chu)   tyo (cho)
    zya (ja)   zyu (ju)   zyo (jo)

Naturally, the change has caused the spelling of certain familiar names of places and things to be altered, for instance:

Old Spelling	New Spelling
Shinto shrine	Sinto shrine
Chion-in temple	Tion-in temple
Mt. Fuji	Mt. Huzi
Chanoyu	Tyanoyu
Chosen	Tyosen
Jujutsu	Zyuzyutu
Jinrikisha	Zinrikisya

CONTENTS

		Page
I.	General Survey of the Japanese Dance	9
	1. Introduction	9
	2. Varieties of Present-day Dance Forms	17
II.	The Kabuki Dance	30
	1. Varieties of the Kabuki Dance	30
	2. The Kabuki Dance and the Music of the Samisen	36
	3. The Stage for the Kabuki Dance	39
	4. Presenting the Dramatic Dance	45
	5. The Kabuki Actor as Dancer	48
	6. Choreographers and Their Schools	52
	7. Education in the Art of Dancing —Some Practical Aspects	56
	8. The Geisya Dance	58
III.	Movements for the New Dance	63
	1. Movements Based upon the Kabuki Dance	63
	2. Movements Based upon the Technique of the Western Dance	67

I. GENERAL SURVEY OF THE JAPANESE DANCE

1. Introduction

Visitors from Europe and America, upon arriving in Japan, will invariably find that their programme contains a visit to the Kabuki Theatre. Those whose special interests are in the artistic features of Japanese life will receive an invitation to the stage dance which the Japanese call *odori* or *mai*, to the performances of Japanese music with the native instruments of *koto* or *samisen*, and to the old Japanese Noh dance or drama. Those who are accorded treatment as national guests will surely enjoy the privilege of witnessing the ancient court dance, known as Bugaku. If it should be in the springtime they will probably be able to see in Kyoto the age-old dance, known as Miyako Odori, better known among tourists from abroad as the Cherry Dance. If they leave the city and go out into the country they may have opportunity to see some of the many religious dances commonly performed at the village Sinto shrines or Buddhist temples. They may see the lion-mask dances in the towns or villages, the Bon dances during the mid-year festival of the dead, or other similar forms of individual or group dancing. To speak of the Japanese dance in general would be to include these and other forms that are to be found widely throughout the Empire.

Miyako Odori or Cherry Dance (half stage on the left)

In Japan the term *mai* or *odori* has been applied to all these dances. Strictly speaking, however, these terms are not identical, the former referring to that quieter type of dancing whose interest lies chiefly in the movements of the hands, while *odori* denotes the dance characterized by swift movements of the feet. The Bugaku and the Noh, to which reference has been made above, and the religious dance known as Kagura, belong primarily to the former group, the *mai* (the verb, *mau*), while the Kabuki dance and the Bon dance are really *odori* (the verb, *odoru*). These two terms, *mai* and *odori*, have, however, been combined and given a Chinese compound pronunciation, *buyō*, so that we now have a general term for all forms of the dance. In our language we have come to use the expressions, Noh Buyō, or Kabuki Buyō. We should

Miyako Odori or Cherry Dance (half stage on the right)

perhaps call attention to an exception in the common use of these terms, a use which sometimes creates confusion in the minds of visitors. There is still a form of dance which is called *mai*, a part of the Kabuki dance, originating in Kamigata. (During the Edo period the cities of Kyoto and Osaka were given this special name, Kamigata, meaing "higher-place," out of respect for the Imperial Court in Kyoto. At the beginning of the Meizi era the Imperial Court removed to Edo, now Tokyo, so that, to be consistent, Tokyo should now be called Kamigata. But, as a matter of fact, the old custom has persisted, and Kyoto and Osaka are Kamigata to this day.) The dance forms that have come from this Kamigata district are of the quieter type, and contain elements of *mai* rather than *odori*; so that they have been and still are called Kamigata Mai. We may understand that the terms *odori* and *mai* have had different connotations in different periods. In this article, however, the term *odori* will be used in its wider sense, including as well the elements of *mai*.

The reason why the Kabuki and the Noh dance are considered to represent the artistic side of Japanese life to tourists from abroad is that they are the characteristic forms of the Japanese dance. Another reason for their popularity among friends from abroad is that their public performances provide comfortable accommodations for the audience and are easily accessible to foreigners. Another point in their favour is that there is no fixed season for their performance, and they may thus be enjoyed by visitors at any time of the year, merely by the obtaining of an admission ticket.

The Kabuki, however, does not consist altogether of dances, the dance in reality forming but one of its elements. But since the Kabuki originated in a dance, and developed its other dramatic forms subsequently, its basic elements are still the movements of the dance. Even today, moreover, the Kabuki programme contains one or two acts of pure dance drama, so that one who is interested in this dance form will find no difficulty in making a study of it.

Somewhat along the line of the Kabuki dance one may see an *odori* performed by geisya girls. These geisya girls are primarily waitresses who attend to guests at banquet halls, whose attentions also include songs and dances to the accompaniment of the *samisen*. They do not usually appear upon a stage, but sing and dance among the guests in the banquet hall or private dining-room.

Zyusuke Hanayagi, choreographer (right) and his pupils

Their dances are, therefore, without stage setting of any kind, or any special make-up; they wear the same clothes with which they have been serving the guests.

Such dances are called *su-odori*, the *su* meaning literally, "just as it is," referring to the wearing of no special dance robes. If one would see these geisya dances he should go to some public eating-house (*ryōriya*), and arrange with the proprietor, there being fixed rates for such performances.

To see the Noh drama one must go to the special Noh theatre during the stated period of public performances. There may be but four or five such performances during the year, and the performance may last for only a single day. They are thus rather rare, and one may not easily be able to witness this form of drama. As far as

Noh dance

the admission ticket is concerned, it may quite easily be obtained by application to such agency as the Japan Tourist Bureau.

The Bugaku is performed only upon special occasions at the Imperial Court. It is, therefore, impossible to witness this old court dance except as such special occasion may offer. It should be noted also, however, that this dance is often performed at the great Sinto shrines at the times of national festivals, at the Meizi Shrine in Tokyo and the Kasuga Shrine at Nara. So that if one does not enjoy the privileges of a national guest at the Imperial Court, he would do well to make use of some national holiday and visit some Sinto shrine where the Bugaku is being performed.

These dances, to which we have here made reference,

Kabuki dance

the Bugaku, the Noh, the Kabuki, may be classified as the artistic dances, while the others, such as the religious dance of Kagura, the Lion-mask dances, the country dances of Bon and Catch-fish may be termed folk-dances. The classification may be easily made along the line of the professional performers, for while the former dances are performed by trained artists of the various schools, the latter are performed by humble farmers or simple men and women. These may take part in the dance as a form of religious service or simply as amusement on festival days or during seasons of leisure in their busy country life. These folk-dances may from the standpoint of the artistic drama seem coarse and vulgar enough, but from that of folklore they often present a most interesting interpretation. These two groups of dances, the artistic and these latter, have had their periods of development in the past, but have equally continued their existence and popularity to this day. Within the larger classification, too, it may be noted that although the Kabuki has been developed through the influence of the Noh drama and the Kagura dance, and the Noh drama through the influence of the Bugaku and the Kagura dance, each has kept its own separate form as well as its own peculiar characteristics. The fact that such a small island Empire as Japan should have perpetuated its art in so many forms, especially in this field of the dance, where we find almost innumerable forms, might be thought to be unique in the world history of art. This may be due to the peculiar national characteristics of Japan, a country which has never been subject to foreign rule, but which has been able to Japonicize all foreign influences introduced, however numerous and however exotic they may have been.

If we take a general view of the Japanese dance we will note that its one outstanding characteristic is what we may call its symbolism. Even though the Bugaku, the Noh and the Kabuki may differ from one another in many of their features, they are all one in the fact that they do not make their dance movement their central purpose. In all three forms of dance, each movement has a definite meaning, and is subject to emotional treatment. This symbolism is more marked in the Noh and the Kabuki dance. In the case of the Noh it becomes quite suggestive, while in that of the Kabuki it is very sensuous. Because of this symbolism the whole composition is much simplified, and through his dress and the objects (fan, towel, etc.) which he employs in his dance, through the bodily movements of the dancer himself, the entire action is made significant. This symbolism which is the very life of the Japanese dance is the one common characteristic of all Japanese dances.

2. Varieties of Present-day Dance Forms

The various forms of present-day dance may be tabulated as follows:

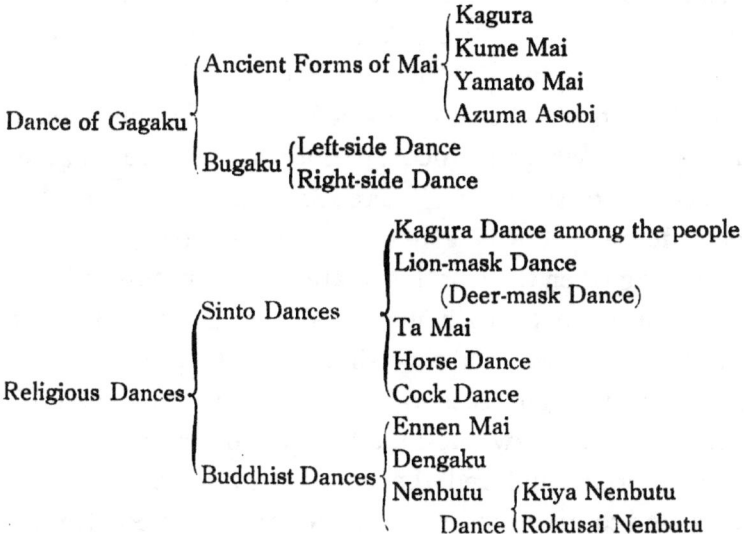

Noh and Kyōgen

Kabuki Dance

Rural Amuse- ⎧ Bon Dance
ment Dances ⎨ Harvest Dance
            ⎩ Great Catch-fish Dance
              Banquet Dances, accompanied with songs

New Dance   ⎧ New Kabuki Dances
Forms   ⎩ Western Style Dances

Our mythology gives us a mystical story of how the dance in this land originated. In the days of the gods and goddesses, so the story goes, Amaterasu-Ōmikami ("Great Heaven-Shining Deity"), greatly incensed at the violence and the ungodly deeds of Susanowo-no-Mikoto, hid herself in the heavenly rock cave. As a consequence the eternal night of darkness prevailed. All the gods were greatly dismayed, and much to their inconvenience all business had to be transacted by artificial light. Thereupon a council of the "eight million gods" was summoned on the dry bed of the "Heavenly River of eight currents," and it was decided that Ame-no-Uzume-no-Mikoto should, in company with other gods, perform an inspired religious dance before the cave. Thereupon Amaterasu-Ōmikami considered, "How is it that the Gods can enjoy such merrymaking when the world is wrapped in darkness as it has been since I shut myself up in this cave!" So saying, she opened the cave door very slightly, and secretly peered out at the joyous scene. Then, as had been planned, Ame-no-Tatikarawo-no-Mikoto opened wide the rock-cave door and induced the goddess to come out of the cave and to occupy the new palace they had constructed for her. This dance, performed by Ame-no-Uzume-no-Mikoto, is said to have been the first dance ever given in Japan.

The Mikagura, ceremonies performed before the Imperial Sanctuary on the occasion of accession to the Throne, or the Harvest Festival, has reference to this rock-cave incident and is said to set at peace the spirits of the Imperial Ancestors. The Kagura music and dance are also performed at various shrines throughout the

Azuma Asobi (right) and Yamato Mai, ancient forms of *mai*

country, and bear among the people the simple name of Kagura, whereas that performed at the Imperial Court is distinguished by the name Mikagura.

The *mai* has existed from the very earliest days of our history in one form or another. The Kume Mai is said to have originated in the day that the Emperor Zinmu carried on the conquest of Yamato, ancient Japan. Other forms with a similar ancient tradition are the Yamato Mai and the Azuma Asobi, preserved in the province of Yamato and the Suruga district (Nara and Sizuoka Prefectures). Of course, these dances have not preserved their original forms unchanged. They were greatly modified during the Nara and Heian periods, the eighth and ninth centuries, through the influence of the Gagaku which was introduced from Korea and China. The importation of foreign music

Bugaku, an old court dance

into Japan dates from the reign of the Emperor Kinmei (the latter part of the sixth century).

The first of these importations was what is now known as Gagaku.* It was later, during the Nara and Heian periods, that the Bugaku came from China, India, Korea and Manchuria. As Imperial patronage was given to these new forms of music and dancing they soon came to be used, not only in Buddhistic services, but also as entertainment in banquet halls in aristocratic homes. And during the Nara period (720-784) new forms were added to the old. These musical forms generally were termed Gagaku, whereas the dances received the name Bugaku. The Gagaku is classified into Uhō, the right side, and

---

* Vide Tourist Library Vol. 15: Japanese Music.

Sahō, the left side. The right side was introduced from Korea and Manchuria, its musical instruments being the *Komabue* (Korean flute), the *hitiriki* (pipe), the *san-no-tuzumi* (hand drum) and the *syōko* (large drum). The left-side music includes those forms which came originally from China and India, as well as those newly composed in Japan. Its musical instruments are the *yokobue* (flute), the *hitiriki*, the *syō* (pipe), the *koto*, the *biwa*, the *taiko* (drum), the *syōko*, and the *kakko* (old drum). These two musical forms of the Gagaku have also the characteristics of right-side and left-side in their dance, or Bugaku. This Bugaku, which had attained its zenith of popularity during the Heian period (784-1192), gradually went into decline as the Samurai rose to political power; and at the close of the Asikaga period, about the fifteenth century, when the century was involved in the throes of warfare, it almost reached the point of extinction. But the Edo period, the seventeenth century, witnessed its revival, and we find it active today. During the Heian period, when the Gagaku was popular, a new Buddhistic form of music called Syōmyō was imported from China. Since that time the Buddhist priests have devised a number of different dance forms based on this music, such forms as are known by the name of Dengaku, Ennen, and others. That which we call Sarugaku came from the Chinese music, Sangaku. These various forms of music and dance achieved an early popularity, and came to be performed quite generally, altogether apart from any special religious or secular purpose. Among the religious dances that are still performed at different places in the country, the most popular are the Kagura and Lion-mask dance.

Miko Kagura, one of Sinto dances

The most common of these secular Kagura are the Sato Kagura and Ō Kagura. Beside these there are the Dai kagura, Zindai Kagura, and Iwato Kagura, but these are more in the form of epithets than any real name to represent any definite character. Some names indicate the place of performance, such as the Yawata Kagura performed at the Yawata Shrine of Iwasimizu in Kyoto, and the Inari Kagura at the Inari Shrine of Husimi in Kyoto. An interesting form of Kagura is that known as the Hiyori Kagura, or the "Fair Day Kagura," so named because it is performed when a newly built ship is launched on some fair day; this is at the Kaisin Shrine of Kagosima Prefecture. There is also the Saru Kagura, or the "Monkey Kagura," so named because, according to tradition, monkeys will come out of the woods and dance to its music, at the Shrine of Sinkumano Sansya-Gongen of Miyazaki Prefecture. In ordinary cases, the Kagura is called by such names as the Seven-fold Kagura, the Twelve-fold Kagura, the Twenty-five-fold Kagura, and the Seventy-five-fold Kagura, according to the number of musical pieces that are performed. The Kagura today is usually performed within the hall of the shrine, but originally it was performed in the open air, on the ground. Some of the Kagura make use of masks, while others do not. That without masks is called *sumen*, a term used also in the Noh play. One of the characteristics of the Japanese dance, as has been noted, is that the dancer manipulates some object in his hand during the performance. This custom came from the Kagura. Such objects, in the Kagura, are called *torimono*. They are ritualistic objects, such as the *sakaki* or evergreen tree, the *hei* or paper decoration, *tue* or staff, *hoko* or halberd, *miki* or libation, and *kagami* or mirror. In their actual use in the Noh and the Kabuki these objects have necessarily undergone some change.

The lion is not native to Japan, but its mask was introduced by the Gigaku, and this form of dance soon displaced what had up to that time been a popular dance, the Deer-mask dance. It should be noted, however, that even today one may see traces of such old mask dances as of the deer, the boar, the dragon, the heron and the cock, in many country places. To pray to the spirit or god of the rice field and then to celebrate the harvest with music and dancing has been quite a common custom from olden times. This harvest dance joined up with certain Buddhistic dances, such as the Dengaku and the Lion-mask dance, and thus has come the present rice-planting dance, the

The Lion-mask dance is very popular at different places

dance that accompanies the prayers for rain. Some festive elements were added to the Kagura when it made its appearance in the country districts, and soon such joyous dance music as Dai Kagura and Sato Kagura took the popular fancy. The principal musical instruments used in the Kagura are the flute and the large drum, to which brass and wooden clappers are sometimes added. For the Lion-mask dance the flute, the drum and the bamboo whisk are the chief instruments. Of these, the bamboo whisk (*sasara*) is most indispensable. In some districts this dance itself is known as "Sasara." Practically the same instruments are used as accompaniment for the Ennen and Dengaku dances.

The dance that is popularly known as Noh* is more

---

*Vide Tourist Library Vol. 2: Japanese Noh Plays.

Dengaku, a form of Buddhist dance

strictly speaking, the Noh of Sarugaku. It originally belonged to the Sangaku of China, and since the Heian period (784–1192) has been performed, along with the Dengaku and Ennen dances, throughout Central Japan, a region known as Kinki. The Noh signifies a performance containing a dramatic plot or story. There was also such a dramatic element in Dengaku and Ennen. But in the case of Sarugaku there was a marked development during the Asikaga period (1392–1573) at the hands of the two geniuses, Kwan-ami the father and Se-ami the son, under the patronage of the Syōgun, Yosimitu Asikaga. These men, by sheer genius, transformed what had been mere folk-dances into a truly artistic dance. After these men there came a succession of able and widely known masters of the Noh, and even through the changes in the Shogunate, from Asikaga to Oda, from Oda to Toyotomi, from Toyotomi to Tokugawa, there was no diminution of the favours bestowed upon the Noh. It was during the last, the Tokugawa period, that it came to be recognized as the ceremonial music of the Syōgun. Before the time of Kwanami and Se-ami the musical instruments of the Noh seem to have been the same as those of the Ennen or Dengaku, namely the flute, the large drum and the various clappers. During this period, however, such harsh and unmusical instruments as the brass and wooden clappers and the wooden whisk were rejected, and the four, the flute, the drum and the large and small hand drums were selected as the musical instruments of the Noh, as they have remained until this day. This choice of instruments has, no doubt, contributed much toward the deep and mysterious spirit which characterizes the Noh.

As the Noh became, during the Edo period, the ceremonial music of the Syōgun, there arose, in competition with this, to meet the popular taste, especially that of the merchant class, a new form of drama known as the Kabuki. The peasant or lower class had remained in a very subordinate position in the life of Japan, from the earliest date down to the Kamakura period, about the thirteenth century. They had but little culture of their own. But during the next century, in the Asikaga period, a new class of people grew up from among the farming population. This was the class of merchants or artisans who were playing their part in the developments of the towns and gaining prosperity from the newly flourishing trade with foreign countries. From the economic standpoint some of them were becoming more powerful even than men of the

Harvest dance is performed to celebrate an abundant harvest

Samurai class. At that time Kyoto and Osaka were the centres of such growth and activity; but when the Tokugawa government was removed to Edo, the present Tokyo, this became the most important town in the land. To meet the taste of these merchants and artisans in such growing towns we find the increasing popularity of the *samisen*, the Kabuki drama and the puppet drama. Thus, in time, the Gagaku came to be regarded as the music of the aristocracy, the Noh the entertainment of the Samurai, and the Kabuki that of the merchants and artisans, each having its own field of activity and patronage. We may say that these three classifications have generally obtained until the present day.

Bon dance is performed as a rural amusement during the festival season for the dead, at the middle of the seventh

Bon dances are usually observed during the festival season for the dead. "Awa Odori" in which the dancers parade through the street (lower)

month according to the lunar calendar. These Bon dances are however, in some places, performed in the autumn, to celebrate an abundant harvest in the farming villages, or a big catch in the fishing villages. They were, no doubt, originally religious dances, but their original purpose has long been forgotten, and they have become merely a form of rural amusement. It must be said, however, that some traces of this former meaning are still noticeable. Among these we might note the Bon dance of Asage village in Simoina County in Nagano Prefecture. Here the primitive form of the religious dance, which it had even before the introduction of Buddhism into this country, is still to be seen. Also there are the Bon dances with different characters throughout the country. The fact that such a variety of these ancient dances should still be performed may be unique in the history of the folk-dance of the world. As these dances are all performed, as a rule, during the Bon season, in July and August, it would require several years for any one person to see them in their native villages. The accompaniment of the dances is not for musical effect in itself, and so has come to be very simple, perhaps the clapping of hands to the accompaniment of a song, or the playing of a flute and the beating of a large drum, and even in rare cases the *samisen*.

Since the beginning of the Taisyō era, 1912, there have arisen various new style dances and the old dances have been influenced by the modern forms. This will be considered further in a later chapter.

II. THE KABUKI DANCE

1. Varieties of the Kabuki Dance

The Kabuki dance, with a history of more than four hundred years, and with a rich variety of artistic element, may be roughly classified under the following four heads:

(1) Kyōgen Zyōruri, or the Dance of Zyōruri
(2) Dance from the Noh Drama
(3) Transfiguration Dance
(4) Comic Zyōruri

(1) The Kyōgen Zyōruri is a dance with a dramatic content. These terms, Kyōgen Zyōruri and Dance of Zyōruri, are synonymous, referring to dramatic dances. There is a very wide variety in these Kabuki dance from the more dramatic Gidayū Kyōgen to the simple Musume Dōzyōzi, a popular dance taken from the Kabuki drama. What are popularly known as *mitiyuki* dances also belong to this group. These *mitiyuki* dances owe their origin to the suggestions of the puppet drama, which developed along with the growth of the Kabuki drama. The characters in these dramatic dances represent themselves as travellers from a certain point to a certain destination. The changing scenes through which they travel are interpreted through the dance and the accompanying music. As these dances are given to interpret scenes they are sometimes given the name *keigoto*, or scenes. Some of

The Dance of Zyōruri from "Seki-no-to"

these *mitiyuki* dances which enjoy popularity today are Imose Yama ("the Man and Wife Mountain"), Senbon Zakura ("The Thousand Cherry Trees"), Keisei Koi Hikyaku ("The Messenger of a Love Letter"). When these *mitiyuki* dances take on the colouring of the Kabuki drama, the characters are quite often made to represent two lovers who have lost their hope in this world, and so are seeking the peace and joy of the other world. They are thus on the journey of death, and during this experience they meet with various personages, all of this being interpreted through the dance. As drama all these are very simple and quite monotonous, but as dancing they provide entertainment for the spectators, who are willing to forego a real plot. Among these representative *mitiyuki* dances we find such as O-Some Hisamatu and Izayoi Seisin.

Mitiyuki dance from "The Thousand Cherry Trees"

(2) Our second group includes the dances taken from the Noh drama. These may be said to belong to the Kyōgen Zyōruri of the first group as far as their contents are concerned, but they find their differentiation from that group in the fact that their materials are largely taken from the Noh, and the stage upon which they are played is constructed in exact imitation of the Noh stage. To this group belong such popular Noh dances as Kanzintyō, Huna Benkei, Ninin Bakama, and Sannin Katawa. These Kabuki dances of the Noh, or originating in Kyōgen Zyōruri, are a modern creation, having first appeared during the Meizi era, since 1868. This recent development is due to the fact, as we have previously indicated, that during the Edo period (1603–1868) the Noh was regarded as the ceremonial music of the Syōgun, and could not be

"Kanzintyō," a dramatic dance adapted from the Noh drama

adapted for use as popular drama or dance. With the dawn of the Meizi era, however, all class distinctions were abolished, and so elements of the Noh drama might be borrowed in the transformation and development of the Kabuki dance.

(3) The so-called transfiguration dances, a term which may at first sight seem rather strange as applied to such dance forms, are those whose motive seems to be the appreciation of dance as its own art, having very little story or plot, and representing a great variety of people, men and women, young and old, of all ranks of society. The dance is, as a matter of fact, a combination of various dances. In a single performance there may often be three, seven, nine, or as many as twelve different dance forms, a dancer making swift transformations of appearance and

Transfiguration dance with seven different forms

character for a variety of impersonations. This rapid change of impersonation and of dance form has given this type of dance the name it bears, of transfiguration dance. At first the transformation was mainly in the matter of changing the character personified or the type of dance, but later it came about that each group of dances was to portray a different age with its own peculiar manners and customs, a thing which in itself would give the dance considerable value. The popular dances of our day, such as Etigo Zisi, Tomo Yakko, Gorō, Asazuma, Huzi Musume, Kamuro, Bunya, Sagi Musume, Sanzya Maturi, and Kakubei, are made by bringing together seven or nine groups of dance forms. These are not always presented in their full form, however, because of their too considerable length, and as the usual thing only certain selections from

Comic Zyōruri dance from "Suō Otosi"

the entire dance are presented.

(4) The comic Zyōruri dances are the Kyōgen Zyōruri, which do have a certain story or plot in them, but we differentiate them from other Kyōgen in the sense that their chief purpose is to rouse laughter and merriment. This is done through the introduction of various comic features, humorous situations and actions, witticisms, puns and jokes. The dramatic dances adapted from the Noh, such as Ninin Bakama, Sannin Katawa, Suō Otosi, and Bō Sibari, some of which have already been referred to, may be classified within this fourth group.

During the Edo period the proper type among all the Kabuki dance forms was the Kyōgen Zyōruri rather than the transfiguration dance, which was at best, as the name indicates, abnormal in character, and one of the by-products of Kyōgen Zyōruri. But today, when we are no longer able to see the old Edo life in its true colours, except through stage performances, these rather abnormal by-products of the past have come to be more highly regarded even than the legitimate child of the art of the Edo period.

2. The Kabuki Dance and the Music of the Samisen*

The chief music of the Kabuki dance is that of the *samisen*. And as there are various forms of the Kabuki dance there are also varieties in the *samisen* music. These cannot be disposed of in a few general words, but merit rather close consideration. The relation between these two, the Kabuki and the *samisen* music, from the beginning of their association, may be briefly stated as follows.

During the earliest period of the Kabuki drama, in the days of its creation, in the age of Keityō (1596), by its originator, O-Kuni of Izumo province, and her followers, these dramas, the Female Kabuki and the Courtesan Kabuki, made no use of the *samisen*. The instruments used in that early day were the Buddhistic gong, and the four that were common to the Noh, as we have described, or perhaps other percussion instruments. But when the Female Kabuki was put under the ban by the Tokugawa government because of its injurious effect upon public morals, and the Youth Kabuki came to take its place in public esteem, the *samisen* was introduced, with the purpose of enriching the musical content of the dramatic productions. From this time on the *samisen* held an im-

---

* Vide Tourist Library Vol. 15: Japanese Music.

Gidayū players occupy the right section of the stage

portant place, not only when the Kabuki was a rather disconnected series of dances, but even more so when these developed into an organized form of drama. And as this form of music became an indispensable part of the Kabuki drama and dance, a group of *samisen* players soon came to be attached to each theatre where the dance was performed. This special form of *samisen* music is known as the Nagauta. Such music has, from the beginning, served as accompaniment for the Kabuki, both drama and dance. This explains why the Nagauta has made such strides in its progress as theatre music. Along with the growth of the Kabuki we see the origin and development of the puppet drama, which also used *samisen* music and songs. This latter music is called Zyōruri, and at first existed entirely apart from the Kabuki music, but later came to be adapted to the Kabuki as well. The most famous form of this Zyōruri is what is popularly known as Gidayū Busi. This last is what we will find in use today in both the puppet drama and the Kabuki drama. Among the musical forms which originated in this Zyōruri and found their development during and after the age of Hōreki (1751) as accompaniment for the Kabuki dance we may mention the Tokiwazu and Tomimoto. It was after the eleventh year of Bunka (1814) that the school of Kiyomoto became powerful. Tomimoto has now almost ceased to exist, but the other two, Tokiwazu and Kiyomoto, together with the Nagauta, are regarded as indispensable accompaniments of the Kabuki dance.

In addition to these Kabuki dances we may see various other dances performed today to the accompaniment of popular songs or of folksongs. There are dances, also, performed to the accompaniment of the *koto*. The music of the *koto* primarily belongs to the blind musicians, who have long regarded it as their right, and such music was never composed with the purpose of being used for a dance. But the very nature of the music produces a certain charm, and gives it a character that is very different from that of other dance music. It presents a special appeal to a certain type of people. In Kyoto and Osaka, especially, since the beginning of the Edo period, dancers not connected with the Kabuki theatre have been fond of presenting their dances to the accompaniment of the *koto*. More recently such dances have been introduced to the Tokyo stage, as well. One outstanding characteristic of the *samisen* music of the Kabuki dance is the clear and resonant sound of the plectrum. Although the *sami-*

sen is a stringed instrument, when the strings are struck the body of the instrument is also struck, so that a mild form of percussion music is also produced. The lines or the figures of the dancers on the stage move or sway in time with the rhythm produced by the sound of the plectrum. This harmony between the rhythm of the plectrum and the dance movement is a vital element in the Kabuki. And the rhythm of the plectrum advances from the weaker to the stronger accent, which is directly opposite to the order that we find in Western music, where the movement is from the stronger accent to the weaker. Some, in their desire to create new forms of the Kabuki dance, have recently tried to use the Western orchestra in place of the *samisen*, but have dismally failed in the attempt to harmonize the rhythm of the Kabuki dance with that of Western music. Such failure may be altogether attributed to this fundamental difference in the nature of the rhythm of these two forms of music. In other words, it is not too much to say that without the music of the *samisen* there can be no Kabuki dance, and the reverse also is true. We thus see that the relation between the Kabuki dance and the *samisen* is vital; one might term each the very life blood of the other.

3. The Stage for the Kabuki Dance

The stage for the Kabuki dance consists of (1) the stage setting, (2) the dress, make-up and personal effects of the dancer, (3) the music at the right wing of the stage.

(1) The Stage Setting

Of all the Kabuki scenes, that of the dance is the most

beautiful. It is bright, like flowers; we may even term it phantastic. The dance stage differs from the ordinary stage of the Kabuki drama. In the first place there is a specially prepared wooden platform upon which the dancer may keep beating time with his feet. Because of this beating upon the platform, a necessary part of the dance, the dancers must always appear upon the stage for the dance with unshod feet. This is true, even when the scene is laid outdoors. Very rarely some such characters as those in Sagi Musume or Sarasi Onna may appear on the stage wearing wooden clogs in order to more fully accentuate their character in the play, but even these must take off their clogs when the dance begins. Even in rain and snow scenes the characters in the Kabuki dance must appear with bare feet or at best in *tabi*, Japanese white socks, with their long robes trailing behind. This is perhaps the most unrealistic or symbolic aspect of the Kabuki dance. A second characteristic of the Kabuki dance stage is the device known as *seriage*, a kind of elevator or lift which may produce a character quite suddenly through a hole in the floor. Such hole may be in the front stage or in the so-called *hanamiti*, a long raised passage which leads to the stage. This last is a unique characteristic of Japanese stage construction. The former type of *seriage*, that in the front stage, is rather complicated and troublesome, and is now seldom used. That in the *hanamiti* is always used with such characters as Tadanobu in Senbon Zakura and Hōkaibō in Huta Omote. There is also another device for bringing a character out upon the stage. This is called *karakuri*. The stage is divided through the middle, and the parts move to the right and left, while in the centre a

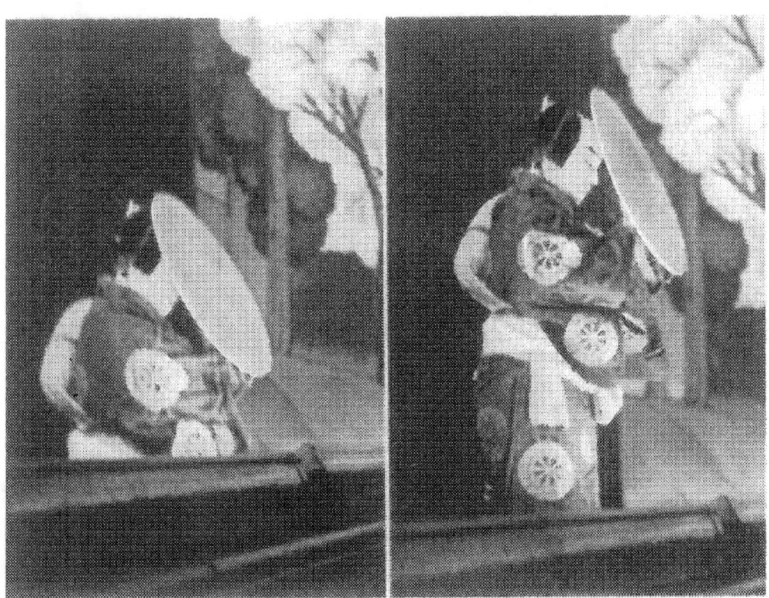

A player makes his appearance through a hole by the *seriage* device

platform moves forward into place, bearing the new character upon it. In such plays as Sikorobiki and Kagami Zisi the dancer comes out upon the stage in this way, on the *karakuri*. The girl character in Sagi Musume appears on the stage by means of what is known as *osidasi syamozi*, a vehicle that is pushed out in place. A third characteristic of the Kabuki dance stage is that the musicians of the Zyōruri or the Nagauta appear upon the stage seated in a row on a large oblong box or platform. This box is always found upon the stage and may be regarded as a regular part of the stage setting.

There are always, also, some branches bearing plum or cherry blossoms, or maple leaves, hanging from the ceiling. These blossoms of the different seasons of the year are made to conform to the time setting of the

Karakuri device for bringing characters out of the back of the stage

drama. Such branches, called *turieda* or "hanging branches," serve as part of the stage setting or decoration, and are quite indispensable to this form of drama. We may state, in short, that the stage setting of the Kabuki dance aims at the creation of a dream-like symbolism, as far as possible avoiding any realism, and thereby enhancing the beauty and charm of this form of the stage.

(2) The Dress, Make-up, Personal Effects

The dress of a Kabuki dancer is very significant, much attention being paid to the figures as well as the colours of the dresses or robes that are worn. The dress, naturally, is designed to accord with the rank and personality of the character that is personified. The dresses and regalia of the Edo period (1603-1868) are commonly in use. There

Turieda or floral curtain representing cherry blossoms

is not, however, very strict adherence to the special age that is being portrayed, in the choice of the costumes. For example, Imose Yama is a story taken from a very early period in our history, the eighth century, but the pretty girl, O-Miwa, in the play, appears in robes that properly belong to the Edo period. It is quite in keeping with the principles of the Kabuki dance that the designs and colouring and figures of the dresses should not be according to reality. As to the dress that is used in the Kabuki dance, there are certain special features that are worthy of note. These are what are popularly known as *hikinuki* and *bukkaeri*. In the former the character appears upon the stage wearing several dresses loosely sewed together. During the performance a simple pulling of a string will be sufficient for the actor to cast off the outer garment and

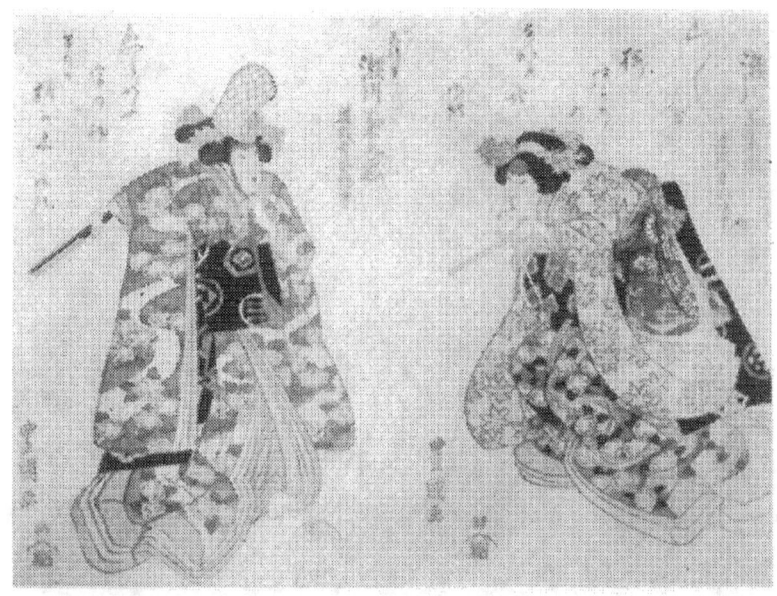

Hikinuki method—a dancer casts away the outer dress (right)

appear in different dress. The name *hikinuki*—pulling out is given to this simple operation. This *hikinuki* method is most effectively used in such pieces as Musume Dōzyōzi and Sagi Musume. *Bukkaeri* is also a method by which the personal appearance of a dancer is changed by the taking off of the upper part of the dress and letting it hang down as the lower dress. In the case of *hikinuki* the outer dress is cast away, but in the *bukkaeri* it is simply turned inside out and allowed to hang. This *bukkaeri* is used in such pieces as Seki-no-To, in which the humble barrier keeper, Sekibei, discloses his real personality by declaring that he is Ōtomo Kuronusi himself and again in Kitune Bi ("the Fox Fire"), where the lady, Yaegaki Hime, is bewitched by a fox.

In the Kabuki the performers often play their part,

holding some object in their hands. This may be regarded as another characteristic of the Kabuki dance. This is true also of the Noh and the Kagura, but is more marked in the case of the Kabuki. The object most often held and most variously manipulated is the Japanese fan. Some dance pieces are specially noted as giving the character the duty of manipulating two fans. Among these are Urasima, Momizi Gari, and Kagami Zisi. While the fan is most often used there are also other objects which frequently have their part in the Kabuki, such objects as the towel, the round fan, the drum with a handle, the toy drum, and various other objects suited to the motif of the drama. As these objects have an important part in enhancing the value of the dance no study of the Kabuki would be complete without giving them due attention.

(3) The Music at the Right Wing of the Stage

The musicians at this end of the stage do not appear on the stage, but are always concealed from the view of the audience, usually by a screen. Hence their music is called, in Japanese, *kage no narimono* ("the music of the shadow"). This music is not performed as accompaniment to the dance, but rather to imitate the more realistic sounds of life. Such music has developed along with the growth of the Kabuki drama, and has been appropriated from that. It is now quite indispensable to the Kyōgen Zyōruri, producing such realistic sounds as the beating rain or snow, or the howling wind.

4. Presenting the Dramatic Dance

One may well ask what the procedure might be of

Dancing with manipulating fans in a scene from "Kagami Zisi'

presenting a dramatic dance piece, from the time of its composition until its production upon the stage. The dance drama is first composed by the author or playwright, and when it has been accepted for stage duty it is handed over to the musician master of Nagauta or Zyōruri, who sets out to create a musical piece that befits the content and the spirit of the play. This operation is, in Japanese, called *husituke*, or "tone-setting." When the musical piece is finished it is played before the *huritukesi*, the choreographer. The work of the dance and music composers is to amplify or interpret the spirit and ideas of the play in the highest musical or dance terms. From a creative point of view their work is but secondary, assisting, as they do, the playwright in carrying out the purpose of his drama. The work of these three artists must be one of cooperation, as their differing contributions are inseparable, and quite essential to a successful result. When the composition is thus fully completed it is given to the Kabuki dancer, trained as he is in the art. If he also approves it he receives instructions from the *huritukesi* as to the best way of performing it. His rehearsals are sometimes directly before the audience.

In former times the choreographer and the actor-dancer were quite often one and the same person. But later, naturally enough, there appeared those who were more skilful in choreography than in actual stage performance, and vice versa, so that such specialization soon began. It is rather interesting to note that the actors or dancers of the stage never trained others in the same art. Perhaps this was simply because they themselves were too busy with their own art to concern themselves with others.

There are today three famous Kabuki dancers who are also actors, Kōsirō Matumoto, Mitugorō Bandō and Hukusuke Nakamura. These have come from families of great dancers, but they have not given themselves to training others than members of their own families. The work of the training of the dancers has always been entrusted to the *huritukesi*. Many famous dancers have come from among the choreographers.

5. The Kabuki Actor as Dancer

For the first hundred and fifty years from the time the Kabuki came into existence, in the seventeenth century, its dances were monopolized by those actors who took the part of heroines in the play. Such actors as Kikunozyō Segawa and Tomizyūrō Nakamura, famous in their female rôles in the Kabuki, during the age of Kyōho and Hōreki (1716-1751) were equally noted as dancers. Their styles in dancing, in such pieces as Dōzyōzi and Syakkyō, have been perpetuated until today. Following in their steps we have the second and third Kikunozyō Segawa and Hansirō Iwai. They are regarded as having been the composers of such popular pieces as Sagi Musume, Ninin Wankyū, and Kurama Zisi. Fom this time on, however, a number of actors famous for their rendition of male parts in the play became equally noted for their skill in the art of dancing. Among these we may mention the ninth Uzaemon Itimura and Nakazō Nakamura, who gave us such masterpieces as Kurama Zisi, Modori Kago, and Huta Omote. During the periods of Bunka, Bunsei and Tenpō, in the nineteenth century, appeared the third and fourth Utaemon Nakamura and the third and fourth Mitugorō

Sixth Kikugorō Onoe (right) in a scene from "Kagami Zisi"

Bandō. Such actors were called *otokoyaku* or *tatiyaku*, those impersonating male characters in the play. Such was their skill and success that it seemed, at the time, as though the art of dancing belonged to the male actors in the play. This proved to be a transitional period, between the golden age of the Kyōgen Zyōruri and the transfiguration dance. Such famous dance pieces as Etigo Zisi, Sio Kumi, Asazuma, Huzi Musume, Urasima, Yasuna, Bunya and Kisen were composed during this period. At this time also appeared the two great actors, the seventh Danzyūrō Itikawa and the third Kikugorō Onoe. It is fair to say that they both showed greater talent as actors than as dancers. But this was the golden age of dancing, and such actors not only made themselves famous by their performances but also left for later age such

Mitugorō Bandō (right) in a scene from "Sanzya Maturi"

masterpieces as Sikoro Biki, Sarasi Onna, Osome Hisamatu and Yasuna. This is a feature of Kabuki which should not be ignored by the student of the art. During and since the Meizi era which followed, we have such representative actors as the ninth Danzyūrō Itikawa, the fifth Kikugorō Onoe and Sigwan Nakamura. Among the masterpieces which Danzyūrō has left us are Huna Benkei, Suō Otosi, Ninin Bakama, Momizi Gari and Kagami Zisi, and to this Kikugorō we are indebted for such plays as Tuti Gumo, Ibaraki and Modori Basi.

Among contemporary dancers the sixth Kikugorō Onoe is generally regarded as the greatest of them all. He was born as the son of the fifth Kikugorō Onoe, and has the enviable distinction of having received careful instruction and training at the hands of that master, the

Ennosuke Itikawa plays a prominent rôle in "Ayaturi Sanbasō"

ninth Danzyūrō Itikawa. His great play, Kagami Zisi, in which Danzyūrō is said to have given him instruction, is regarded as his masterpiece, unequalled among all Kabuki dance pieces. His versatile talents are given free play in pieces he received from his father, such as Tuti Gumo, Ibaraki and Modori Basi, in pieces from Danzyūrō, such as Huna Benkei, Momizi Gari, and Suō Otosi, not to mention such other popular pieces as Dōzyōzi, Sagi Musume, Asazuma and Huzi Musume, in all of which he plays the rôle of heroine. Among his own compositions we might make mention of Migawari Zazen, Bō Sibari and Tati Nusubito. Not far behind Kikugorō we should place Mitugorō Bandō, whose artistic style must be termed classically correct, to the minutest detail. His superb skill is best shown in his joint performances with Kikugorō, in such pieces as Sanzya Maturi, Migawari Zazen, Bō Sibari and Tati Nusubito. Kōsirō Matumoto is well suited for his rôle as a tragic hero, with his imposing figure and his deep sounding voice. Perhaps his most masterly presentation is that of the character Benkei, in the popular drama, Kanzintyō. Next in order would come Ennosuke Itikawa, who plays a prominent rôle in such lively pieces as Ayaturi Sanbasō and Ren Zisi. He is regarded as a pioneer in certain fields of Kabuki art. Among other contemporary dance actors who enjoy popular esteem we should name Sōzyūrō Sawamura, Syōtyō Itikawa, Hukusuke Nakamura and Dansirō Itikawa.

6. Choreographers and Their Schools

The composers of the Kabuki plays and their dances have not usually, as we have earlier noted, themselves appeared on the stage, but have had the privilege of training the actual performers in the rôles that they themselves had created. This custom had its part in the development of schools of dancing, a feature which should be of special interest to the student of this form of art.

The first choreographer of the Kabuki dance is said to have been Mansaku Sigayama, who was attached to the Nakamura Theatre in Edo. He later changed his name to Denzirō Nakamura, and became the founder of the Sigayama School. This new type of school had its beginnings in the age of Kyōho (1716). This school was maintained by his descendants for several generations, but finally lost its place of leadership during the age of Tenmei (1781) when we have a group of new choreographers appearing upon the scene. Among these we should name

Senzō Nisikawa and Kanbei Huzima, founders of the schools that bear their names. These Nisikawa and Huzima Schools, as well as the Sigayama, have survived until today. There was a time when the Nisikawa School declined and ceased its activity; this was in the age of the third Senzō Nisikawa. But a student named Kansuke, of the third Kanbei Huzima group, revived it in the age of Bunsei (1823) and took his place as the fourth Senzō Nisikawa, a choreographer of great capability and a special favourite of the seventh Danzyūrō. He is said to have composed the dance of Kanzintyō. Among the students of this Senzō there were two specially able choreographers, Toranosuke and Yosizirō. After the death of Senzō, Toranosuke moved to Nagoya, taking the name of Koisaburō Nisikawa. Yosizirō also adopted a new name, that of Zyusuke Hanayagi, and became founder of the school that bears this name, which continues until this day. In the 36th year of Meizi (1903), a student of the Hanayagi School, Yosimatu by name, left that school and founded a new one to which he gave the name, Wakayagi, himself taking the name Zyudō Wakayagi. The third Huzima having no male heir, succession passed on through the female line, but this disqualified the family for being ranked as a first-class choreographer. Thus the school gradually lost its place among the choreographers, the Nisikawas and the Hanayagis easily holding the supremacy here. During the latter part of the Edo period (1603-1868), however, there appeared among the followers of the Huzima school a very able choreographer with the name of Kanemon Huzima. By the aid of the ninth Danzyūrō he took an outstanding position as choreographer for a leading

Kabuki theatre, becoming a rival of Zyusuke Hanayagi. The famous Kabuki dancer of our day, Kōsirō Matsumoto, is the adopted son of this Kanemon Huzima. Zyusuke Hanayagi, of the rival school, was succeeded, after his death, by his own son Yositarō, who has become the second Hanayagi, and is today a most popular choreographer of the Kabuki dance. The Wakayagi, though founded as one of the recognized schools of choreography, has abandoned theatricals, and is now exerting its energies along the line of the training of geisya dancers. As to the Nisikawa School, after the death of the fourth Senzō, it was greatly overshadowed by its chief rival, the School of Hanayagi, and in Tokyo has lost its place as choreographer at the Kabuki Theatre. The Nisikawa branch school at Nagoya, however, has been able to maintain its prestige, even though the main school in Tokyo has gone into decline. Mention should also be made of the School of Bandō, whose founder was a student of the third Mitugorō Bandō in the latter part of the Edo period. He was specially favoured in receiving the patronage of the ladies of the Tokugawa family, enjoying the privilege of training students, even though he did not attach himself directly to any of the Kabuki theatres. He has many followers today, the present Mitugorō Bandō being regarded as their leader. In addition to these, reference might be made to such schools as those of Itiyama, Mizuki, Nanaōgi and Syōga, but these would hardly be regarded as rivals of those mentioned above.

  Even from the above brief statement one may readily understand that these choreographic schools have not been based upon any definite artistic form, neither have they kept themselves strictly to any specially long line of tradition, even though their names have been perpetuated until today. The special characteristics of the various schools have not been rigidly maintained, but have been subject to various changes from generation to generation. The line of their development has been laid out more by the masters themselves than by the traditions of the individual school. For example, Kansuke Huzima who became a master of the art through the tutelage of Kanbei Huzima, was to be the one to revive the Nisikawa School, himself to become the fourth Senzō. One might figure out that his characteristics consisted of those of the third Kansuke Huzima, plus those of his own individuality, having no characteristics whatever of the second and third Nisikawa Schools. A similar statement might be made in the case of Zyusuke Hanayagi, who carried with him, with no loss or modification, the characteristics of the Nisikawa School, when he changed his name Yosizirō to Zyusuke Hanayagi, and succeeded to the leadership of the Hanayagi School. It may be affirmed therefore that what we term schools were not in the real sense schools of this art, but rather names given to designate the position which these artists held in society.

Another peculiar custom which has survived until today, may be here mentioned, as we conclude this section. It is that these *huritukesi* (choreographers) other than actors, have been content to be merely the dancing coach, without themselves appearing in that rôle upon the stage. As might be expected they are sometimes overurged to perform in private, but on such occasion they wear no dancing dress or make-up of any kind, but present the

At the studio of Zyusuke Hanayagi

dance in *hakama*, the Japanese ceremonial skirt, or in *suodori*, as it is called. This may be attributed to the deference that came to be paid to the actors during the times when they came to perform their art independently of the professional dance actors.

7. Education in the Art of Dancing — Some Practical Aspects

Speaking generally, art education in Japan has been based chiefly upon the principle of intuition. It has been the method of encouraging students to find their way through their own individual abilities rather than for the instructor to inculcate his own ideas into the pupil's head. It may be thought of as somewhat along the line of the training of a genius. There was no systematic education

Training of little girls at the studio of Sumi Hanayagi

which would impart knowledge, for instance, based upon minute scientific analysis such as that we see in Western countries today. This was especially true in regard to the training of dancers during the Edo period. During those days the students of this art received private lessons from their masters, and if they proved to have talent they in their turn came to be masters of the art. As far as training methods were concerned there was but little difference between the training of dancers and of artisans. Artisans imparted their knowledge and skill to their apprentices by employing them in their business for a number of years. The training of dancers was accomplished in much the same way. No provision was made, for instance, for any public school where any definite knowledge or practice of the art might be scientifically planned. The students of

∼57

this art were trained in private lessons given them in the home of the master. And only those were received as students who could show promising ability, and who declared their intention of devoting their lives to such professional art. Such might be admitted as pupils on the payment of a proper fee.

For example, when a student of the Hanayagi School wishes to establish himself as a professional under the name of Hanayagi, he must first receive the recommendation of the master, and then be granted some special name (first name) somewhat similar to Hanayagi or Zyu-Hanayagi. In this way the school is able to keep its unity as well as its own peculiar style and characteristics. In more recent times, however, along with the appearance of new schools of dancing, provisions have also been made for public schools of this kind.

8. The Geisya Dance

The relation between the Kabuki dance and the dance of the geisya girls has been quite close from a very early day. In a sense the dance of O-Kuni, who originated the Kabuki drama, as well as that of the Female Kabuki, was a geisya dance. We recall that in the sixth year of Kwanei (1629) the Female Kabuki was put under the ban by the government of the time because of its unwholesome influence upon the public morals of the day. There has never been any connection between the geisya dance and the Kabuki since that time. The Kabuki has been limited to male actors, who even on occasions are required to perform in the rôle of women. The Female Kabuki, however, had been created to meet a normal

Geisya girls entertain guests with dancing

need, and even though by law it was swept from the legitimate stage, it could not be completely eliminated. It soon came to find its expression in those professional girls whose function was to entertain the guests at banquets with music and dancing. This was not a surprising development in the course of social life. Different terms have been applied to these girls who are trained to entertain guests in banquet halls. In Kamigata, that is, Kyoto and Osaka, they have been called *geiko*, and in Edo, now Tokyo, the name *odoriko* has been used. The term geisya was formerly used to include not only the professional girls, but also such men as played the *samisen*. Later it came to be applied to the girls only. At that time these men were able to dance and to play the *samisen*. Such men as were able to both dance and play the *samisen* came to be called *hōkan*. This is true even today. The question is sometimes asked as to how these geisya girls are trained in the art of dancing. They usually receive their professional training from the masters of the regular dancing schools, or from some other professional dancers. As was stated in a former section, those who attain proficiency in the art are permitted to call themselves by the name of the school in which they have received their training. This was true of the geisya as well as the Male Kabuki dancer. However, it is rather unusual for them to call themselves by the name of the school as long as they are geisya. The schools most popular among the geisya girls are those of Hanayagi, Huzima and Wakayagi. It is fair to say that it is because of their intimate connection with the geisya class that these three schools hold such an important position in society and wield such power in the world of dancing.

The dances performed by the geisya girls are usually from the Kabuki. These dances are performed, however, without any stage setting or special dancing robes. The ordinary geisya dress is worn. The dances themselves are of different kinds. Some would be such pieces as pertain to some auspicious occasion or happy event that is being celebrated. There are those lively, quick tempo, marchlike pieces that are supposed to inspire merriment in the hearts of the guests. Sometimes the party will make a request for folksongs or other popular airs, which the geisya is trained in offering. In addition to these dances which are performed before the guests with the *saké* cups, there are more formal dances, given twice each year, in the spring and the fall. These dances are an exception to

Azuma Odori, a favourite spring dance in Tokyo

the rule that we have stated, and are given with stage setting and with dress and make-up like that of the Kabuki actors. These famous annual performances are given on a grand scale in the cities of Kyoto, Osaka and Tokyo, the most famous of all being the Spring Dance. Perhaps the oldest of these is the Miyako Odori, better known abroad by the name of the Cherry Dance. This is performed throughout the month of April each year at the Kaburenzyō Theatre in Gion, Kyoto, a theatre erected by the Geisya Union for this express purpose. This has been an annual affair, without interruption since its beginning in the fifth year of Meizi (1872). In the same city there is another annual performance for a month, beginning in the first of May. This is called Kamogawa Odori, and is performed by the geisya girls of Ponto Tyō. In Osaka we find what is known as Naniwa Odori, performed at Kitano Sinti. Though this was the earliest of the Osaka performances, its beginning was ten years later than that of Kyoto (1882). It was suspended for some years, but was revived in the fourth year of Taisyō (1915) and since then has had its annual show without interruption. This also is given for one month, beginning with the first of May, and is the last each year of the Osaka spring performances. A more recent spring dance of this kind in Osaka is the Asibe Odori at Nanti, which began in the twenty-first year of Meizi (1888), and performs its annual dance for one month from the first of April. Still later in point of origin we have the Naniwa Odori of Sinmati, Osaka, dating from the forty-first year of Meizi (1908), and offering its dance for one month from the first of each April. The first of these dances to be given each spring, however, is the Konohana Odori at Horie, Osaka, beginning its annual thirty day performance on the fifteenth of March.

In Tokyo such performances have been given by the geisya girls of Sinbasi or Yanagibasi since the beginning of the Meizi era. The favourite spring dance in Tokyo is the Azuma Odori, which gave its first performance on the completion of the Enbuzyō Theatre in April of the fourteenth year of Taisyō (1925) and whose popularity has continued undimmed.

III. MOVEMENTS FOR THE NEW DANCE

1. Movements Based upon the Kabuki Dance

With the Restoration of 1868, due to the merits of the great Emperor Meizi, Japan was awakened from her dream of feudalism which had reached its highest development during the Edo period (1603-1868) immediately preceding. From that day to this there has been a rapid development in every sphere of her national life, in thought, education, science, industry, due, for the most part, to the influence of Western civilization. More especially after her victorious wars with China (1894-1895) and with Russia (1904-1905), she made great strides in the path of progress, so that it seemed as if everything Japanese was to undergo a complete change, and the characteristics of the Edo period lost forever. Limiting our observation here to the sphere of art, we can see that it was only natural that, even though the Bugaku, the Noh and the Kabuki forms of drama might be highly valued by some and might be preserved, still there would be more and more demand that new dance forms be created to represent the new national life of the new age. Even to this day the moot question in the dancing world has been whether the new dance movements should be essentially of the old Kabuki type or should be based entirely upon the technique of Western art. Much study has been given to this question, and much data of interest and

—63

value is offered to the student of this art in Japan.

The pioneer in the movement for that type of reform which would build upon the old Kabuki dance—though his work did truly have a large part in the general development of the art—was Syōyō Tubouti (1859-1935). His essay entitled "The New Musical Drama," published in the thirty-seventh year of Meizi (1904) is a clear and complete statement of his ideas as to the purpose and method of the new movement. His own dramatic compositions, Sin Urasima, Kanzan Zittoku, Ositi Kitisa, Onatu Kyōran and others, were of high enough value to remedy the deficiencies in the old Kabuki drama. But there were no others of equal ability and enthusiasm to join Syōyō in this reformation movement, either in the music, the dance composition or the actual performance, the root, the trunk or the branch, shall we say; so this movement never advanced far beyond the bounds of the old Kabuki dance, after all. We should add, however, that this tree of his planting and tender care did begin to bear fruit during the Taisyō era, from 1912. Several artists appeared with the desire and the ability to carry forward his purpose. Among these was Sizue Huzikage, then known as Sizue Huzima, whose first performance in the sixth year of Taisyō (1917), under the auspices of the Tōin Society, gave great impetus to the revival of the movement. Her contribution consisted, not in the creation of a highly deveploped new dance, but in breaking with the traditions that had held the old Kabuki in their grip, preventing the introduction of new dance forms. She was a dancer and could accomplish many things that Syōyō the scholar could not be expected to accomplish. She was an able

A scene from "Sibon," composed by Sizue Huzikage

disciple of Kanemon Huzima, the famous dance master whose influence was unmatched during the Meizi and Taisyō eras, supported as she was by the ninth Danzyūrō Itikawa. She herself had once been a geisya. She was the first to break with the old tradition that no woman should perform this dance in dancing dress in public. Moreover she composed her own dances, a thing hitherto permitted to be done only by the recognized masters. Defying the long time custom of preserving the characteristics of one school, and thus securing its unity, she performed before the public the dances that she herself had composed. Among her compositions of historical significance and of the new classical spirit the best known is her new interpretation of the classical Midare Gami Yoruno Amigasa. Noteworthy also is her adaptation from a Chi-

"Rhythm of Drums," a representative art of Tamami Hanayagi

nese drama, known as Sibon(1921). This emancipation of female dancers, brought about by the originality and courage of the gifted Sizue, has produced a long succession of such dancers, through the Taisyō and Syōwa eras, until our day. Among the famous names of such dancers and their schools we should note Tamami Hanayagi and her Tamami Kai, Sumi Hanayagi and her Akebono Kai, Kinko Hayasi and her Ginsen Kai, Harue Azuma and her Syuntō Kai, Kansoga Huzima and her Motome Kai, and the second Zyusuke Hanayagi and his school, Hanayagi Kenkyū Kai. From this school have come such present-day favourites as Tamami Hanayagi and Sumi Hanayagi. Perhaps the former of these two would be accorded the palm as the most popular artist of this type of today, with her new technique and her outstanding ability. She has

Performance by Baku Isii and his pupils

been able to introduce into the execution of her dance a new life and expression, something never witnessed in the old Kabuki dance. Her best known pieces, representative of her art, are "The butterfly," somewhat after the style of the Bugaku, and "The rhythm of drums," her own interpretation of an old folk-dance.

2. Movements Based upon the Technique of the Western Dance

The introduction of the technique of Western dancing into Japan dates from the forty-fifth year of Meizi (1912) when a Musical Comedy Department was established in the newly opened Imperial Theatre in Tokyo, with an Italian, G. V. Rosi, as instructor. The time was evidently too early, however, for the popularity of musical

Takarazuka girls performance

comedy among the Japanese people, and this department was very short-lived, being dissolved soon after its organization. Among the students of Rosi there was a number of able dancers, such as Baku Isii, Masao Takata, Seiko Hara (later Mrs. Takata) and Kunihiko Nanbu, all destined to have their part in carrying on the development of this new dance which was just beginning to attain popularity. Baku Isii joined the New Theatre which had been organized by Kaoru Osanai in the fifth year of Taisyō (1916), and there performed such compositions as "A page from my diary," "A story," and "Light and darkness" by Kōsaku Yamada, the well-known music composer. At a later date Isii appeared with Masao Takata in the theatres of Asakusa Park, in furtherance of this new movement. Still later, after both had returned from abroad

Syōtiku girls' performance

where they had had opportunity to study their art in Europe and America, they created their own special forms of the art. Isii was more influenced by the French dance, while Takata leaned toward the ballet, the opera and the music hall dance. Unfortunately, however, Takata died while still quite young. His work has been carried on by his wife, Seiko Takata. Among other contemporary dancers of this school mention should be made of Takasi Masuda, Takaya Eguti, Misako Miya, Yosio Aoyama and Sai Syōki, upon whose shoulders now rests the future of this youthful art.

More recently, to meet the popularity of jazz and the revue show, there has come into existence a combination of the ballet and the old Kabuki dance, the Kabuki revue, which is attracting its crowds of devotees at the Takarazuka Girls' Opera Theatre and the Syōtiku Girls' Opera Theatre. The former was established for purposes of popular entertainment at the Takarazuka Hot Spring by the Osaka Express Electric Company in the third year of Taisyō (1914). This form of opera has steadily grown in popularity. The Syōtiku Girls' Opera was created to meet such demands, and is drawing its crowds, eager to enjoy this new art of the Syōwa era.

(204 L 22-2038)

ODORI (Japanese Dance)

日本舞踊

昭和十三年三月廿五日印刷　　國際觀光局
昭和十三年四月一日發行

　　　　　　　　東京市麹町區丸ノ内一丁目
發行兼　　　　財團
印刷者　　　　法人　國際觀光協會

　　　　　　　　宮　部　幸　三

　　　　　　　　東京市牛込區榎町七番地
印刷所　　　　大日本印刷株式會社
　　　　　　　　　榎　町　工　場

　　　　　　　　丸　善　株　式　會　社
發賣所　　　　東京市日本橋區通二丁目
SELLING　　　MARUZEN CO. LTD., TOKYO
AGENTS　　　ジャパン・ツーリスト・ビューロー
　　　　　　　（日　本　旅　行　協　會）
　　　　　　　　　　東　京　驛　内
　　　　　　　　JAPAN TOURIST BUREAU
　　　　　　　　　　　　TOKYO

定價金五拾錢

For Product Safety Concerns and Information please contact our EU
representative GPSR@taylorandfrancis.com
Taylor & Francis Verlag GmbH, Kaufingerstraße 24, 80331 München, Germany